Music for Royal Occasions

Celebratory music from more than 500 years of royal ceremonies.

Published by
Novello Publishing Limited
14-15 Berners Street,
London W1T 3LJ, UK.

Exclusive Distributors:
Music Sales Limited
Distribution Centre, Newmarket Road,
Bury St Edmunds, Suffolk IP33 3YB, UK.

Music Sales Corporation
257 Park Avenue South,
New York, NY 10010, USA.

Music Sales Pty Limited
20 Resolution Drive, Caringbah,
NSW 2229, Australia.

Order No. NOV292952
ISBN 978-1-78038-587-7

Music processed by Paul Ewers Music Design.

Printed in the EU.

www.chesternovello.com

Behold, O God our defender

Composed for the Coronation of
Queen Elizabeth II, 2 June 1953

Psalm 84: vv 9-10

Herbert Howells

bet - - - ter than a thou - - sand,___

bet - - ter, bet - - ter than a

bet - - - ter, bet - - ter than a

- - ter,___ is___ bet - - ter than a

___ one__ day in thy courts_____ is bet -

thou - - - - sand,___ is bet -

thou - - - - sand,___ is bet -

thou - - - - sand,___ is bet -

6

Christmas Day, 1952

Birthday Song for a Royal Child

Composed for the birth of H.R.H. Prince Andrew
19 February 1960

C. Day Lewis

Arthur Bliss

ring _____ With roy - al gold _____ of daf - fo -

14

16

Blest pair of sirens

Performed at the Marriage of His Royal Highness Prince William
of Wales, K.G. with Miss Catherine Middleton, 29 April 2011

John Milton

C. Hubert H. Parry

A

21

Allegro

F SOPRANO

mf dolce

O may we soon a-gain re-new that song, And keep in tune with

mf *p*

poco cresc.

heaven, and keep in tune with heaven, till God____ ere long To His ce-

ALTO

TENOR

mf

O may we soon a-gain re-

BASS

O

poco cresc.

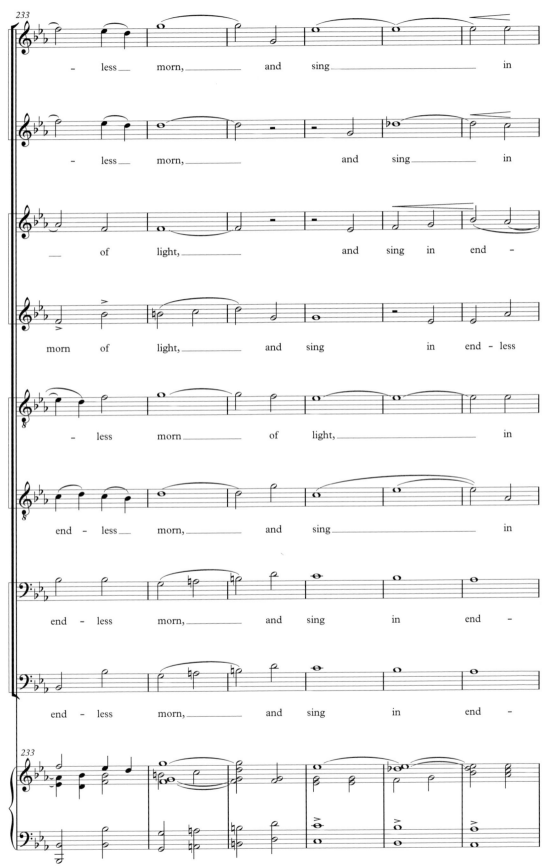

50

sing in end - - less morn of light.

sing in end - - less morn of light.

sing in end - - less morn of light.

sing in end - less morn of light.

sing in end - less morn of light.

sing in end - less morn of light.

sing in end - less morn of light.

sing in end - less morn of light.

Confortare

Composed for the Coronation of
Queen Elizabeth II, 2 June 1953

George Dyson

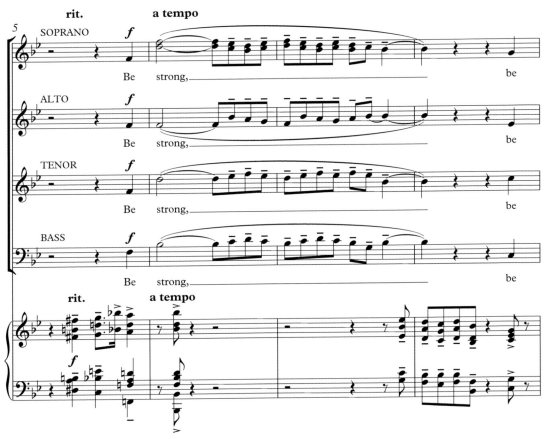

I was glad

Composed for the Coronation of
King George IV, 19 July 1821

Words from Psalm 122

Thomas Attwood

PIANO

58

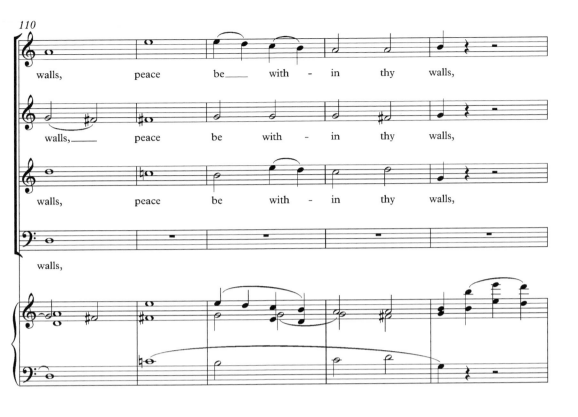

walls, peace be with - in thy walls,
walls,___ peace be with - in thy walls,
walls, peace be with - in thy walls,
walls,

peace be with - in thy walls, peace
peace be with - in thy walls,___ peace
peace be with - in thy walls, thy
peace be with - in thy walls, thy

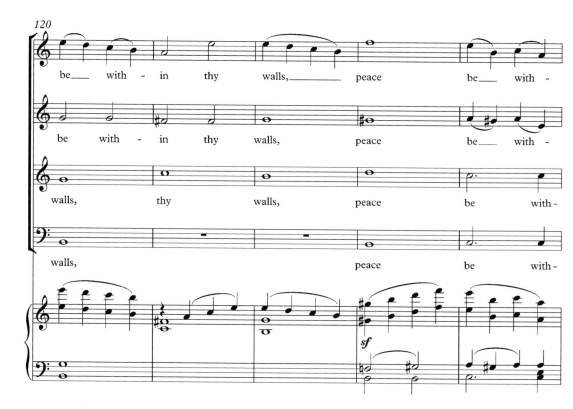

138

pa - la-ces, with - in thy pa - la-ces.

pa - la-ces, with - in thy pa - la-ces.

pa - la-ces, with - in thy pa - la-ces.

pa - la-ces, with - in thy pa - la-ces.

più moto.

143

I___ was___ glad___ when they said un - to me: We___ will

I was glad when they said un - to me, they said: We will

I was glad when they said un - to me: will

I was glad when they said un - to me, they said: We will

più moto.

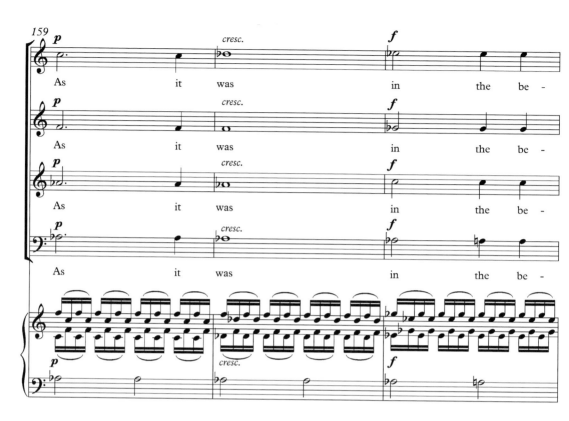

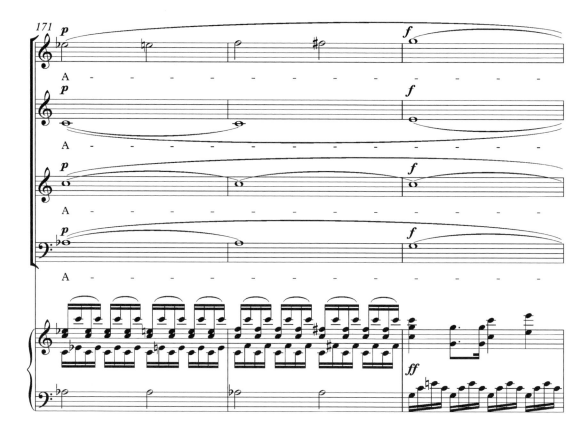

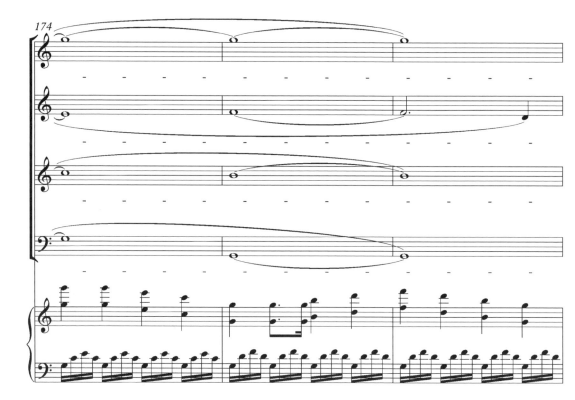

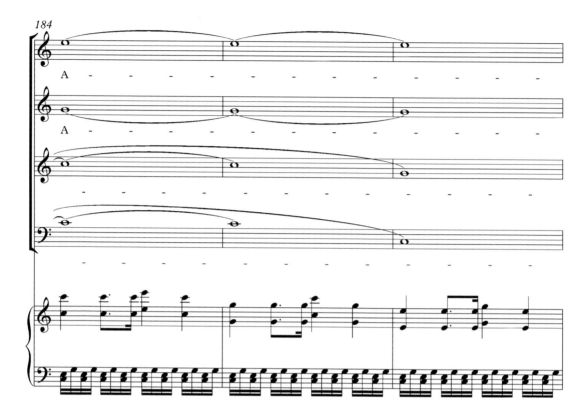

I was glad

Composed for the Coronation of
King Edward VII, 9 August 1902

Words from Psalm 122

C. Hubert H. Parry

78

80

Queen's Scholars of Westminster School

Vi – vat Re – gi – na!

Vi – vat Re – gi – na E – li – za – be – tha! vi – vat! vi – vat! vi – vat!

* When the traditional 'Vivats' are impracticable a cut can be made from * to letter **G** on page 212.

† A Fanfare may be interpolated here if required.

Slower
FULL CHOIR

Vi-vat Re - gi-na! Vi - vat Re-gi-na E-li-za - be-tha! vi-vat! vi-vat!

Vi-vat Re - gi-na! Vi - vat Re-gi-na E-li-za - be-tha! vi-vat! vi-vat!

Vi-vat Re - gi-na! Vi - vat Re-gi-na E-li-za - be-tha! vi-vat! vi-vat!

Vi-vat Re - gi-na! Vi - vat Re-gi-na E-li-za - be-tha! vi-vat! vi-vat!

Slower

vi-vat! vi - vat!

vi-vat! vi - vat!

vi-vat! vi - vat!

vi-vat! vi - vat!

Allargando

FF **Più lento**

dim.

I was glad

Composed for the Coronation of
King James II, 23 April 1685

Words from Psalm 122

Henry Purcell

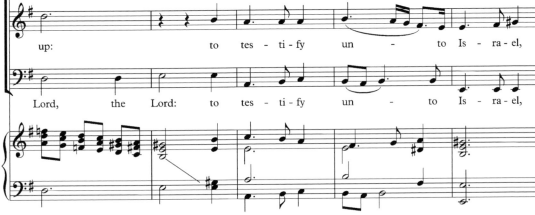

Let my prayer

Composed for the Coronation of
Queen Elizabeth II, 2 June 1953

William H. Harris

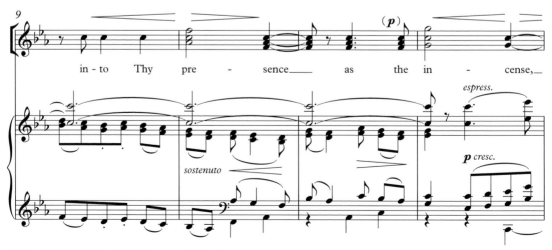

O hearken thou

Anthem, arranged from the Offertorium
composed for the Coronation of King George V
and Queen Mary, 22 June 1911

Psalm 5: vv 2-3

Edward Elgar, Op. 64
Edited by Bruce Wood

O Lord, grant the King a long life

Composed for the Coronation of
King James II, 23 April 1685

Psalm 61: vv 6-7; 132, v 19

William Child

Rejoice in the Lord alway

Performed at the Coronation of
Queen Elizabeth II, 2 June 1953

Philippians iv: 4-7   Anonymous (mid-sixteenth century)

Dedicated to
Their Royal Highnesses The Duke & Duchess of Cambridge
with respectful good wishes

Ubi caritas

Composed for the Marriage of His Royal Highness Prince William of Wales, K.G. with Miss Catherine
Middleton and first performed by the Choirs of Westminster Abbey and Her Majesty's Chapel Royal,
St James's Palace, conducted by James O'Donnell, at Westminster Abbey, Friday, 29th April 2011.

Paul Mealor

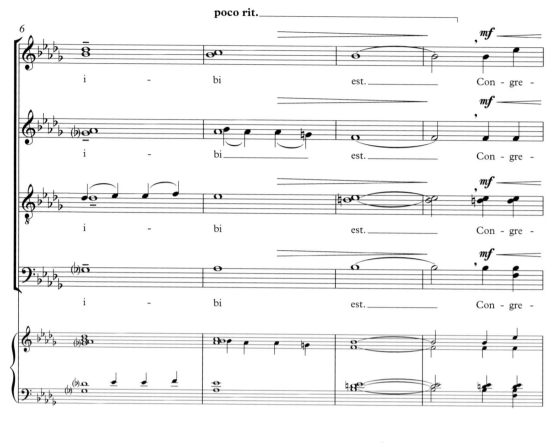

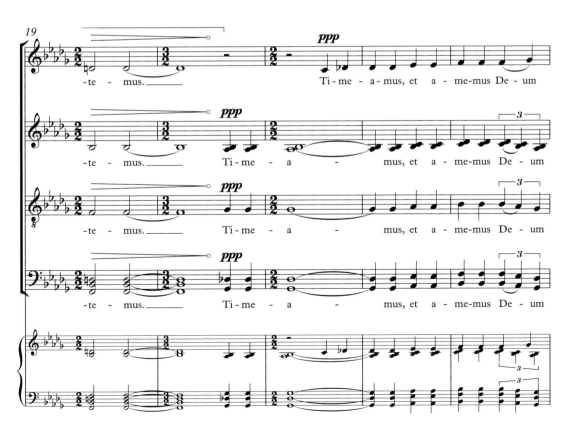

* Bracketed notes are optional divisi.

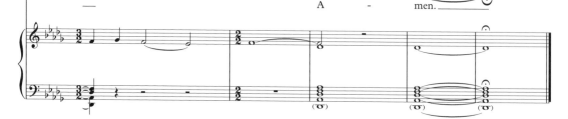

Zadok the priest

Composed for the Coronation of
King George II, 22 October 1727

1 Kings 1: 38-40

George Frideric Handel

Chorus - "Zadok the priest"

Andante maestoso

PIANO

Chorus - "And all the people rejoic'd."

Chorus - "God save the King."